PARENT
Care

by
Woodrow Kroll and Don Hawkins

BACK TO THE BIBLE®

PARENT CARE
published by Back to the Bible
©1998 by Woodrow Kroll and Don Hawkins

International Standard Book Number
0-8474-1473-6

Edited by Rachel Derowitsch
Cover design by Laura Goodspeed

For information:
BACK TO THE BIBLE
POST OFFICE BOX 82808
LINCOLN, NEBRASKA 68501

1 2 3 4 5 6 7 8—04 03 02 01 00 99 98

Printed in the USA

CONTENTS

◆ ACKNOWLEDGMENTS ◆

Special tribute is due to our parents, Frank and Betty Kroll and Jim and Juanita Hawkins. Had they not cared for us as they did, we would not have learned the importance of extending care to them.

We also wish to thank Beki Garrett for her diligence in typing and retyping the manuscript; to Dawn Leuschen for coordinating the project; to Allen Bean and Martin Jones for providing us with extensive research and resources; to Rachel Derowitsch for her editorial expertise; to Laura Goodspeed for layout and design work; and to other members of our Back to the Bible ministry team, including our printing department, for their various contributions.

THE 1
Sandwich Generation

Few of us expect to gain life-changing insight while standing at the counter of a McDonald's restaurant, but it can happen. When the young counter attendant charged me (Don) only a quarter for a cup of coffee, I asked why, since the posted price was 50 cents. The young lady explained, "It's the senior's rate."

Who could she possibly be talking about? I wondered. *Maybe she's nearsighted.*

Less than a week later, after I had spoken in the morning service in our church here in Lincoln, Nebraska, someone told my wife, Kathy, "You must have married an older man."

To be candid, both of the authors feel young and energetic. We are both physically active, blessed with good health and possess all our mental faculties (although some of our colleagues might disagree at times). We travel a lot, are engaged in extensive ministry, enjoy our children and grandchildren and try to help care for our parents.

But the fact is we're growing older.

Statistics indicate that the American population of those over 50 will grow 11 percent by the year 2001. Those in the 50- to 64-year-old subgroup we fit into, the group we refuse to label "young seniors" because we'd rather not use the "s" word, will increase by 19 percent during that same time.[1] Remarkably, another individual turns 50 every seven seconds in America.

Meanwhile, as modern technology stretches our lives to even greater lengths, many of us find ourselves—and our parents—growing older in relatively good health. According to the *Oxford Book of Aging*, "For the first time in human history, most people can expect to live into their seventies in reasonably good health."[2]

Parents and Children

As our children grow up and we and our parents grow older, it seems the problems we face become more complex each year. Many of those problems involve the fact that we find ourselves "sandwiched" between caring for children who are practically grown and providing care for our parents as they age.

Today there are 30 million Americans who are 85 and older. By the year 2000, experts estimate there will be 7 million of these "oldest old." While medical breakthroughs such as knee and hip replacements will allow millions to lead healthy, vigorous lives into their 90s, many of them will require longer and more intense care than has been true in previous decades. About 30 percent of this group have been diagnosed with Alzheimer's disease. Twenty-four percent already live in nursing homes.

Most of those who are not living in nursing homes will still require significant care from children who themselves are elderly, or from other care givers.[3]

As we began research at Back to the Bible in preparation for launching *Confident Living for Midlife and Beyond*, our new ministry targeted to those 50-plus, we discovered that nearly one out of every four American households, or more than 22 million families, currently provides informal care to a relative or friend age 50 or older. This number will increase dramatically as the elderly population doubles during the next several decades. (Couple this with the fact that disability rates among those 65-plus are falling—a 15 percent decline between 1982 and 1994.[4]) Today there are 70 million Americans age 50-plus, with another 70 million right behind them. The extra 15 or 20 years we have gained in our life spans have been added to the middle of our lives rather than the end.

Two factors have resulted from this, both affecting the economy significantly. First, those 50-plus hold the purse strings to a $1.6 trillion pocketbook. The purchasing power of this group is projected to grow by 29 percent over the next decade.[5] Meanwhile, there is additional demand and growth in the assisted living industry. The three largest providers in this field have announced plans to add at least 100 properties each by the year 2000. Don Sapaugh, president of Premier Behavioral Healthcare Services in Houston, Texas, notes that there are four major options available for parents who need care.

"The first line of action for many people today is adding an additional bedroom onto their home for elderly family members. Secondly, there are assisted living centers, which are sort of halfway between living in your home and a skilled nursing facility. With this option, a degree of nursing services is often provided. If physical needs require it, the next option is a rehabilitation center, which offers extensive medical assistance on a short-term basis. A fourth option is a long-term residential care facility or nursing home."

According to Sapaugh, since this segment of the population suffers from a greater proportion of mental health problems than any other segment, mental health care is another concern. Options include outpatient centers, home health care, partial hospitalization and inpatient psychiatric facilities.

As Sapaugh explained, there are different levels of assisted living available.

"It's really based on the type of care that is required by the individual. They do a complete assessment, physical, emotional, relational. They determine the financial ability of the individual who needs to be placed in that setting, and then they determine to what degree they require nursing care at an assisted living center. But you try to give them as much independence as possible without actually incurring the exorbitant cost of a skilled nursing or nursing home."

One of the important decisions to make is whether to purchase long-term care insurance, since one of the most significant issues facing many of us today involves financing the cost of long-term health care. Recent studies estimate that 43 percent of people aged 65 will enter a nursing home at some time, and many more will need long-term care at home. And half of those who enter a nursing facility will likely stay for at least a year. Given the increasing life span and the growing elderly population, many families are likely to face a financial crisis of staggering proportions.

Since a year's stay in a nursing home can cost between $50,000 and $60,000, and the average length of stay is three years, many middle-income families could see their life's savings wiped out. Medicare covers only short-term rehabilitative care, and Medicaid, the last resort for those who become impoverished, appears to be in danger of collapsing under escalating demand.

Yet according to one survey, 76 percent of the respondents said they did not expect to need long-term care in the future.[6]

While today's long-term care policies are probably of higher quality than those in the past, prospective purchasers need to be well informed in order to secure the best possible coverage for their circumstances. Long-term care insurance is probably best explained by someone who specializes in this complex product. Factors to consider include the following:

• benefit eligibility requirements—for example, is medical necessity a factor?

• coverage for mental or nervous disorders

• coverage for custodial care—the most common kind received by nursing home or retirement facility patients

• home and community care—are individuals covered who do not enter a nursing facility, but who prefer to draw upon the wide range of home care services available?

• cost and value
• deductibles
• the renewability of the policy

Remember that everyone's needs are different. No single plan is best for everyone.

In the following chapters you will learn how both of us (Woodrow Kroll and Don Hawkins) have been confronted with the need for additional care for our parents as they grow older. Yet as we noted after a recent prayer time at Back to the Bible, we are not alone in facing this issue.

Dave Hansen, our vice president of International Ministries, and his wife, Judy, have devoted a great deal of time and energy to caring for Judy's parents, who have spent much of their lives on a farm near a small community in eastern Montana.

Marvin Carr, our director of General Services, and his wife, Donna, moved Donna's parents in with them nearly four years ago. When health issues led Donna's mother to choose to enter a nursing home, Marvin and Donna continued to care for her father, now nearly 94, in their home while visiting Donna's mom virtually every day until her death last July.

Cherry Thompson, in our Accounting department, also faced the agonizing decision of placing her mother in a nursing home. You'll read more about the trauma of that decision and the extended effort Cherry and her family put into her mother's care.

Janet Miller, executive secretary to two of our vice presidents, became aware of her mother's problem with Alzheimer's less than a year ago. But as Janet noted, "She's progressed to the stage now where we are talking about putting her in a nursing home sooner rather than later." Complicating the decision for Janet and her brothers and sister is the need to provide additional care for her 85-year-old father.

Beyond Our Ministry

Of course, the problem of caring for parents as they age extends far beyond Back to the Bible's offices in Lincoln, Nebraska. Sue Severin, a 57-year-old health educator in San Anselmo, California, started an Alzheimer's support group for adult children after her mother was diagnosed with the disease. Severin says, "My mother hasn't known who I am for years; I can't remember the last time I was her daughter. She used to hit and bite and kick me, and I would cry most of the way home. It was so terrible to see her. Then there's my father, who has become more depressed, and . . . has no social life. No friends come to visit . . . . It's horrifying. They're your parents."[7]

Sue first noticed the problem in 1989 while attending a Christmas party at her parents' home. She began driving up to Atherton during the week and realized just how bad off her mother was. As she put it, "The house was dysfunctional. The refrigerator full of doggie bags. And my father was in total denial even though he showed me a note my mother had written in 1986 saying, 'Something is happening to me. I'd rather die than end up a vegetable like my mother.'"

Sue's first two steps were to "learn all I could about the disease, and . . . [persuade] Dad to get mom's name off legal papers where she could do damage."

The cause of Alzheimer's is unknown, although it appears that heredity is involved in 10 to 30 percent of the cases. Currently there is no known cure for it, and relatively few of its symptoms respond to treatment except for the depression that frequently accompanies this disease. Alzheimer's usually follows a 6- to 20-year course. Approximately 10 percent of the 65-plus generation may have Alzheimer's, and as many as 47 percent of those over 85 are likely to be experiencing some stage of the illness.

For many caregivers, the problem involves an increasing burden coupled with an unwillingness of other siblings to help. A recent letter to Ann Landers read,

"This is for all the sisters and brothers of caregivers who are too busy with their own lives to lend a hand.

"Four years ago my life changed when my mother became ill with a progressive disease. I put all my plans on hold and little by little gave up visiting my friends and doing volunteer work, socializing, attending night school and spending time with my husband. I must now use all my free time to take my parents to their doctor's appointments and tend to their needs. I'm not complaining—my parents are wonderful people, and I consider it a privilege to care for them. But I am upset because my siblings do nothing to help me.

"In the beginning my brother and sister bombarded me with questions about 'the folks' but now after almost five years, they never ask how Mom and Dad are getting along nor do they offer to give me any relief. I don't think I should need to hire a stranger to take care of my parents, but it looks like I may have to . . . my life is so stressful right now that my health is suffering."[8]

In her response, Landers observed that this is a story heard far too many times. She explained to "No Name" that although "there is no way you can force your siblings to step up to the plate and give you a hand," they need to be told of the needs, and if they refuse to help, either other family members need to be enlisted or outside assistance must be secured and the financial implications addressed.

The financial issue is no small matter either. When Diane Cevolani's dad, a retired shipfitter and widower, was diagnosed with lung cancer, his slow death took him from middle-class status to welfare applicant almost over night.[9] According to Cevolani, her sister and brother-in-law began providing care in their nearby home. Nurses' aides were hired to take up the slack; then with costs and stress escalating, the family made the difficult decision to put him in a nursing home. "We went through twelve thousand dollars in the blink of an eye," Cevolani explained. "Before long we had exhausted his entire eighteen thousand dollars of life savings. Then we applied for Medi-Cal for Dad."

The day after Diane had spent several hours applying for Medi-Cal assistance for her father— a process she described as "degrading"—her dad died.

Similar stories have been told by countless families. After all, helping an aging parent—or perhaps a grandparent, aunt or uncle—can be complex, expensive and confusing. For some, the issues are relatively minor. Perhaps a mother needs more help cleaning or cooking. But often minor needs escalate into major issues, even incapacitation. A family may be faced with the sudden, shocking blow of a stroke, heart attack, cancer or similar trauma.

In the next two chapters, we will explore our own stories. Then we'll return to the nature of the challenge itself, a biblical perspective, our own emotions and some practical steps to take—and to what to avoid—in providing parent care.

[1] *Guerilla Marketing Newsletter*, April 28, 1997.

[2] Thomas R. Cole and Mary C. Winkle. *The Oxford Book of Aging* (Oxford, N.Y.: Oxford University Press), 1994.

[3] "Over Eighty-Five Population in U.S. to Double by 2020," Robert Rosenblatt, *Los Angeles Times*, May 21, 1996.

[4] *The Maturing Marketplace*, April 22, 1997.

[5] *Guerilla Marketing Newsletter*, April 28, 1997.

[6] Harry Crosby, *Should I Buy Long-Term Care Insurance?* (Colombia, S.C.: Harry Crosby, 1997).

[7] *The Electric Examiner*, HTML Agent 8:14:51, April 2, 1995.

[8] "Siblings Not Helping With Aging Parents," Ann Landers, *Lincoln Journal Star*, Nov. 25, 1997.

[9] "Middle Class to Welfare in the Blink of an Eye," *Electric Examiner*, HTML Agent 1:16:52 PM, April 4, 1995.

THE 2
Kroll Story

I come from a family of long livers. I know that sounds like a line from Henny Youngman ("Take my wife, please!"), but I mean that many of my ancestors lived into their 80s and beyond.

My paternal grandfather and grandmother, Andrew and Mary Kroll, lived long enough to celebrate their 73rd wedding anniversary. Later that year he died, just short of his 98th birthday. She lived a short time longer, dying at age 91.

We often think of people in Bible times as living incredibly long lives. Adam was 930 years old when he died. Noah lived to be 950 years. And Methuselah was the granddaddy of them all, living until age 969. But those life spans decreased dramatically as sin began to take its toll on the human race. Abraham lived for 175 years (Gen. 25:7). By the time of Moses, a life span was down to 120 years (Deut. 34:7). And, remarkably, David lived to be only 70 (2 Sam. 5:4). My grandparents beat him by a mile.

My grandfather was a tailor in the "old country." He came to the United States at age 19 and found work, not in the garment district of New York, but as a hand on a farm in western Pennsylvania. This young tailor's life soon changed dramatically. First, he learned to love the land and work with his hands. And second, the farmer's wife had a younger sister who recently had come to America to live with them. Andrew never got over the farm, or the young sister. He married Mary Bulas and they began their 73-year life together. Couples standing before the wedding altar today could learn a lot from my grandparents.

The Simple Life

My Grandpa and Grandma Kroll farmed most of their lives. It was a simple life, but a good one. They were country people, very hard workers. Every month or so they would go into a tiny town with the unlikely name of Zelienople to buy supplies.

Then, when my grandfather turned 65, a strange thing happened. His neighbors came by and said, "Well, Andrew, I guess you'll be retiring now." My grandfather questioned, "Why?" The farmers said, "Because this is America. Everybody retires at 65 in America." It sounded good to him, so my grandfather sold the farm and retired.

A short time later the neighbors came by and said, "Well, Andrew, I guess you'll be moving to Florida now." My grandfather questioned, "Why?" The farmers said, "Because this is America. Everybody moves to Florida when they retire."

So, at age 65, after living on the farm all those years, my grandparents moved to Miami. There they lived in the hustle and bustle of the city until they died.

As my grandparents aged, the quality of their life decreased. They spent their last years in a tiny mobile home with a cabana attached to the side. As I remember, the cabana was bigger than the trailer.

When my family and I attended their 73rd wedding anniversary, we went to visit my grandparents as soon as we arrived in Miami. As we walked to the cabana, my grandfather came out to meet us, hobbling along with his cane. By this time, his hearing was severely impaired and his eyesight was nearly gone. I'll never forget his greeting. He threw his arms around me, kissed me on each cheek, squinted his eyes and said, "Who are you, anyway?" He could barely see me, but he knew family was coming and that made it all right.

A "Can-do" Pastor

I've reflected on that greeting over the years. *Surely*, I thought, *losing your eyesight, or your hearing, or your ability to move about with ease was the worst loss associated with aging.* But I was wrong. While my grandfather's body was showing his age, his mind was not. He retained good mental ability up to the day he died. His son wasn't so fortunate.

My father was a pastor. He successfully pastored the same church for 33 years. He was a hard-working pastor, a very unusual pastor. His heart was as big as I've ever seen. He was the kind of man for whom almost nothing was an obstacle. If it needed to be done, he'd find a way to do it.

Once our youth group needed transportation to a national convention, but the church had no money. So my father bought a bus and took the teens to the convention. I don't mean a rickety old school bus; he bought a Flixible coach, then the equivalent of a Greyhound bus.

On another occasion when the church needed more space for Sunday school rooms, the deacons of the church decided to raise the church, dig out a basement and return the building to its foundation. But, again, there was no money. So my father bought a bulldozer and did the work himself. As a young boy, I thought my father could do anything.

At the time of this writing, my father is 83 years old. His years of ministry are over. He served long and well. I'd like to say that all he has left are his memories, but he doesn't even have all of them. My dad has Alzheimer's disease, and much of his past is gone from his mind.

When I compare the later years of my grandfather and my father and think about my own future, I find myself praying, "Lord, take my eyes and ears if you must, but please let me keep my mind until I draw my last breath."

A Bewildered Family

Alzheimer's is cruel. It robs its victims of life before life is over. It is a slow death, with its victims dying thousands of days before their final day. It's not only a personal difficulty; it's a family disaster. It affects the spouse and children as much, and many times more, than it does the person with the disease. As a family we were bewildered at what we saw happening right before our eyes. It couldn't be true; it couldn't be happening; it couldn't be happening to us! But it was.

This chapter is the story of my family and our personal struggle with Alzheimer's. It's the story of my dad and mom, an unusual pair of faithful servants. It chronicles their good times and bad times as my father struggles with Alzheimer's. It is not his story alone, because families—not individuals—deal with Alzheimer's. This is as much Mom's story as his.

On November 16, 1990, a convocation was held in Lincoln, Nebraska, during which I was installed as the third General Director and Bible Teacher of Back to the Bible. There was an impressive assortment of radio and ministry personalities there, but the one whose presence meant the most to me was my father. He gave the dedication prayer as the others gathered around with their hands upon me.

It was here that I began to suspect something might be wrong. My father decided to say a few words before he prayed, "because it's my son and he can't stop me." At the time I thought the confusion in his remarks was due to nervousness. Now it appears more likely that it may have been the first evidence of Alzheimer's. It would be several years before we knew for sure.

In May 1993, my youngest daughter, Tiffany, graduated from high school. Her grandma and grandpa flew to Nebraska to join in the festivities. My father had always been able to do just about anything with his hands. He was a skilled craftsman with wood. While they were visiting us, my wife, Linda, asked Dad to install a shelf above her range for a microwave. It was a simple task—but not for him. My father measured the space for the shelf, then measured it again and again. In fact, he measured it for more than an hour, but he couldn't interpret what the measurements meant. And when it was time to attach the shelf, he stared at his hammer, and screwdriver, and rule and drill. He couldn't remember which tool he needed to screw the shelf to the wall. Linda and I looked at each other with teary eyes. Something was happening to our father.

Suspicions Confirmed

There is usually a defining event that confirms all suspicions of Alzheimer's. For my father, that defining event involved a surgery that took place on April 4, 1995.

My mother needed a second knee replacement and my father had been having difficulty with his hip. My brothers and I live hundreds of miles from their town in western Pennsylvania. My older brother and his wife—Jerry and Linda—live in Virginia. My younger brother and his wife—Ron and Kathy—live in Florida. Linda and I live in Nebraska. We knew neither of our parents could take care of the other after a surgery, so we arranged for their surgeries to occur together. That way we could take turns caring for them at the same time. My sister-in-law Linda nursed them along the first two weeks after their surgery. My wife took her turn the next two weeks. The next week and a half Ron and Kathy were there.

After their surgeries, my mother recovered wonderfully. My father did not. Physically he was fine; mentally he was a different man. He told everyone who visited him in the hospital that the reason he was in there was because he had been mugged in the parking lot. Sadly, he believed that was true.

His demeanor in the hospital was not that of my pastor/father. He would not stay in bed; he would not listen to the nurses; he would pull out tubes and disconnect monitors. Finally he had to be restrained. His anger level rose dramatically. He complained about almost everything— and that certainly wasn't my father. He had become that stereotypical elderly male patient, at the end of the hall, crying out and complaining about everything. His personality had changed dramatically.

We spoke with his family physician and related some earlier instances of what appeared to be aberrant behavior. The doctor invited a neurologist and a psychiatrist to evaluate him. After a CAT scan and a series of other tests, they concluded that my father was suffering from Alzheimer's disease.

"Who's That Outside My Window?"

A few days after my father was released from the hospital, his doctor started him on 10 milligrams of Cognex. He also began treating him for depression with Paxil. Adjusting to these medicines wasn't easy. As the dosage of Cognex increased, so did his nausea. Often he complained of being too sick to eat or even get out of bed. To what degree the sickness was real we don't know, but it was real to him.

Everything seemed to trouble my father at this point. He had continual difficulty with his hearing. He had worn hearing aids for many years, but now there was the added frustration of not understanding how to work them. He wouldn't talk to us on the phone because "all the buzzing" irritated him. There was a switch on his hearing aids to control the volume, as well as to turn them on and off. Although he now suffers from 70 percent hearing loss, most of the time when he couldn't hear it was because he had turned his hearing aids off instead of on. He just didn't understand, and what's worse, he couldn't be made to understand.

Paranoia began to torment him. He insisted that my mother keep all the windows locked. She could never open any of them, regardless of how oppressive the heat became in the summer. Their home was not air-conditioned. My father constantly saw a face outside of the windows looking in. He was certain there was someone there. The drapes had to be drawn throughout the house every night. Fortunately, that period of paranoia has now passed, and even though the windows have to remain shut and locked, he no longer sees people outside.

My father's understanding and memory continued to fail. His inability to follow the story line on a television program, combined with his inability to hear well, meant that passing the evenings by watching television was not an option for him. There were two exceptions, however. My father has never been interested in politics, but increasingly he began watching C-Span for hours. When he became bored with that, he'd watch the Weather Channel. We knew it wasn't an interest in government or changing weather patterns that intrigued him. It was a non-threatening, non-thinking companionship.

These programs demanded nothing of him. They simply left him alone.

"I'm Sure I Paid That Bill"

At this point, things began to fall apart rapidly for my dad. He had always handled the family finances, wrote all the checks, paid all the bills. But suddenly things were so confusing. Bills were not being paid. He began to accuse the banks of hiding his money or not giving it to him when he wanted. When we questioned him, he didn't know how much money he had in his checking and savings accounts. He never entrusted my mother with family financial matters. She could have handled it easily, but she never had and it was all new to her.

Shortly after Christmas 1995, Linda's father became ill. His illness was diagnosed as a fast-growing cancer. We flew to Pennsylvania in January 1996 to be with him and shortly thereafter, February 11, he died. We returned to Pennsylvania for the funeral and spent a week with our family there.

Since we don't often get "home," we decided to take a part of that week and help my parents assess their finances. In my dad's safe we found canceled checks dating back to the 1940s. There were other documents that were horribly out of date. My parents had life and other forms of insurance, but neither of them knew where their policies were or how much insurance was in force. We called the companies and had duplicates of the policies mailed to us.

We knew my parents had some retirement money invested in certificates of deposit, but they didn't know how much or what banks held them. We investigated and had them consolidated to one bank so every other month one of the CDs matured. That way, if they needed the money they could reclaim it without penalty. We also discovered Dad had a savings account at another bank, containing several thousand dollars, that my mother didn't even know about. We transferred those funds to an account with a higher yield.

My father was willing to accept our help. He agreed with all that we suggested, but was unwilling to throw anything away. We placed hundreds of useless papers and canceled checks in brown grocery bags and he took them to the basement to discard them. After we were gone, he returned most of them to the safe.

It was evident that the family finances were now beyond his ability. My mother had to take over. That was hard for my dad, but he agreed— and then refused to help. If he wasn't going to do it, he wasn't going to help her do it either. We got her started, showing her what she needed to know. And with occasional telephone calls to my brothers and me for clarification or advice, she has done well.

"I Might As Well Be Dead!"

With his diminished abilities came greater despondency. He couldn't use his tools, tools my dad had mastered over the years and tools he loved so much. He couldn't balance the checkbook. He no longer understood anything remotely financial in nature. Sometimes a check would arrive at the house and he would "file it away," which means it would never be found again. His depression grew, often to the point of serious concern. A number of times I've heard him say, "I can't get my words out. I can't remember anything. Everybody thinks I'm a dummy. Life isn't worth living anymore. I might as well be dead."

Of the many things I have seen Alzheimer's do to my dad, perhaps the worst is the way it has robbed him of himself. He is not the same man I have known all my life. He is angry, often childish, sometimes even a threat. He still prays, he still attends church, he still reads the Word, he still retains the hope of life eternal; but life here and now is very different for him. He's not enjoying life the way he did. Before the disease, my father never would have said, "I might as well be dead." But Alzheimer's has robbed him of being the man he was.

We took these veiled references to suicide seriously. My father had some guns and a few rifles from World War II. We got rid of them. We hid a couple of his prized war relics in the attic just in case we had to produce them someday to show him. He was getting more despondent all the time. But things would get much worse.

"Who's That Guy Who Keeps Going Upstairs?"

It was no longer safe for my mother and father to be alone in their home. But because they had built their house in 1939, shaking heaven and earth would not get him to move out now. Dad saw no need for any form of in-home care, and he certainly saw no need to move to a smaller house, apartment or retirement facility. Meanwhile, he couldn't or wouldn't help my mother with the housework because "men just didn't do that sort of thing." The burden of his care was increasing and he didn't know it. It was left to my mother. Something had to be done.

Near the end of 1996 the church that my father had pastored for so many years was searching for a part-time youth director. The congregation was looking for a young couple with no children who could give impetus and direction to their youth outreach. After the search process, the couple whom the church finally called was Matt and Tina Work. That in itself was a truly amazing answer to prayer. You see, Matt is my son-in-law and Tina is my daughter. Someone from the family would live close enough to check on my parents.

But God's answer to prayer was even greater than we assumed possible. God always does "exceedingly abundantly above all that we ask or think" (Eph. 3:20). My parents' house was quite large, which presented a problem for my mother to clean. It was a lovely country home with lots of room. There were three huge bedrooms and a bath upstairs that hadn't been used in years. Matt and Tina had been married only two years and needed an economical place to live. They weren't going to make much money at the church anyway. Problem solved. Matt and Tina moved in upstairs and are now there, in the evening hours and through the night at least, to watch over my parents daily.

But even this remarkable answer to prayer was not without its problems. Alzheimer's not only robs the mind of memory but often produces childlike behavior. Even though my dad knew Matt, he often would say to my mother, "Who's that guy who keeps coming into our house and going upstairs?" At other times he acted as if he had known Matt forever.

Strangely enough, Matt presented another challenge in the home. Suddenly there was another man in the house. "Why was he here? What did he want? Was he trying to take over? Is he moving in on my wife?" As odd as it may seem, all these questions surfaced in my father's mind. I'm grateful to Matt for showing the maturity of character to be confronted with some of these questions without complaint or response.

"I Can Drive Better Than Any of Them"

A few paragraphs back I said things would get worse for my father, and they did. Everyone in our family knew his driving wasn't as safe as it should be. We talked with the doctor about it, but it seemed as if everything else had been taken away from my dad. The things he enjoyed most in life he no longer could comprehend, let alone do. He was stripped of his personality, stripped of his pride, stripped of his abilities. There was only one thing left that gave him a sense of control—driving his car or pickup. The doctor was cool to the idea of denying my father the privilege of driving.

But his driving was a threat to himself and those around him. In April 1997 Dad drove down a one-way street the wrong way and was stopped by the police. The officer was extremely kind and very gentle, but told my father he may be notified that he would be required to take a driver's test. My dad was devastated. "They all think I can't drive anymore. They think I'm a dummy. I can drive better than any of them."

He had always been a safe, good driver. But his mind was playing tricks on him. Once when my brother Ron was riding with him in my dad's pickup, Ron said, "I saw my life flash before my eyes a dozen times." Apparently my father pulled into a lane of oncoming traffic several times.

In August 1997, the State of Pennsylvania sent a notice informing Dad that he must surrender his driver's license for medical reasons. The letter said that if his medical condition improved and the doctor notified them, the state would review his case and he could have his license back. My brother Jerry had the unenviable task of explaining this final blow to my father's manhood. Initially he seemed surprisingly accepting, but there have been frequent flare-ups of anger and determination that he would drive regardless of what anyone said. He hasn't because my mother and Tina have been able to talk him out of it.

Where Are We Now?

As of this writing, my parents are still living at home, although we have continually encouraged them to move in with one of their sons. We also have tried to keep other options open for them. We have taken them to visit retirement centers and lifecare facilities. Once, after touring a facility here in Lincoln for an hour, my father, who had been bent over walking with his cane, asked Linda what that place was. When she responded that it was a place for people to live who needed a little help, he straightened right up and literally ran down the hall to prove to us he didn't need to be in a place like that.

Matt and Tina are still living above my parents at home. My father's medicine has been changed to 10 milligrams of Aricept, a new treatment that seems to be better for him. There are fewer delusions since he no longer takes Paxil for depression, and less nausea since the change from Cognex. He continues to have good days and bad days. There are days that every little thing angers him. Other days he is tender and kind, like the father we all remember.

In many respects, Alzheimer's returns a person to childhood—behaviorally, attitudinally and emotionally. Jealousy, anger, impatience, paranoia, selfishness and stubbornness are all common among victims of this disease. My father has experienced all of them, most of which were totally foreign to him before.

When his anger rises or anything threatening comes, he retreats to the safety of his bed. It's not uncommon to see my dad in a fetal position in bed until the middle of the afternoon. When he is up it's an exciting hour of C-Span or a nap in his favorite chair.

The most alive I have seen him in the last few years was on a visit here to Nebraska some months ago. Linda wanted me to build some wooden storage shelves in our garage. My dad went to the lumberyard with me to get the materials. On the way home, with the back of the van open and the windows down, I looked over at him and he was like the family dog, riding with his head out the window, the wind blowing his hair and a huge smile on his face. It was seventh heaven. His mind was wandering through a meadow of fond memories. He was excited and happy. He was useful. He was working with wood again.

Once during the construction project I slid a hammer over to him and nonchalantly said, "Drive a few nails in that end to hold it down." I looked away immediately to express full confidence in his ability. The man who used to drive an eightpenny nail with 3 hits took 15 to put this one away, but I have not seen him happier in a half dozen years.

Continuing Concerns

As a family, our concerns for my father are actually exceeded by our concerns for my mother. She bears much of the verbal and emotional stress at home. She is strong and loving and understands that much of what my father says does not come from his heart, but it's still hard. Convincing him that he is demanding more of her than she is able to give has not been easy. But if Mom were not at his side, he would need 24-hour care. She gives him his medicine. She convinces him to get up and shower. She prepares all the meals for him, except when Tina is home early enough. She gives round-the-clock care, and this is taking its toll on her.

The day will come, perhaps soon, when we will have to override Dad's will to preserve the quality of her life. It has not been easy watching what Alzheimer's has done, because it has taken a toll on both of them. My brothers and I have had amazing unity as a family, but we continue to take our cues from our parents on what they want, what they think they can handle.

For years I have taught the wonderful truths found in 2 Corinthians 5:17: "Therefore, if anyone is in Christ, he is a new creation; old things have passed away; behold, all things have become new." I have seen that happen spiritually to hundreds of people. I never thought I would see an emotional and mental change in the reverse direction. But with my father's Alzheimer's, I have seen the closest thing to an emotionally new man I may ever experience, and I don't like what I see.

For him, in the last five or six years, everything has changed. His lifestyle, his daily habits, his interests, his demeanor—all things have changed, but not for the better. The most comforting thing is the absolute assurance that what is eternal cannot change. My father's eternal salvation will not change. His eternal destiny will not change. One day his body will change, but for the better. Now things are not changing the way we want, but our family is confident of better things ahead.

For years we all needed him. My dad was our strength. He was the can-do pastor. He was the hardworking father. He was all his sons ever wanted him to be. Now, he needs us. We need to be strong for him, and for my mother, and by God's grace we will be. We pray to that end every day.

THE 3
Hawkins Story

The hills appeared ablaze with various shades of red and orange as my plane banked into its final approach to the Birmingham airport. I was en route to a speaking engagement, and something of even greater personal importance—a meeting with my two brothers and two sisters to discuss present and future care options for my parents, both of whom are approaching 80 years of age.

Mother and Dad have been blessed with health and strength. Both came to know the Lord as Savior in 1952, just before I made that decision as a child. Dad and I were baptized the same evening at Westwood Baptist Church in Birmingham.

Dad began a 42-year career with the Southern Railway, shoveling coal as a fireman. One of my earliest memories involves seeing him perched beside a steam engine, a big smile on a face streaked with soot from the coal, the huge steam engine puffing and belching like some prehistoric monster.

During World War II, Dad served in the U.S. Marines. He spent several years in the Pacific theater, primarily involved in aviation repair and maintenance, part of the famous "Black Sheep Squadron" of Colonel John "Pappy" Boyington.

Mother and Dad met through Dad's sister Margie. Mother and Aunt Margie worked together as legal secretaries in a law office in Birmingham. Mother had the incredible ability to type nearly 100 words per minute on an old Royal manual typewriter.

Although Dad worked long hours with the railroad, making freight and occasional passenger runs from Birmingham to nearby states, he and mother made our spiritual growth a priority. Dad had become a firm believer in what he called the "family altar," and whether he was home or not, evenings were marked by reading Scripture and praying. Faithful church attendance also was an important part of our family regimen. In addition, I was encouraged to attend Christian camps. Each summer at camp played a key role in my spiritual development.

My Grandparents

Both my parents became involved in caring for their own parents. The final years of all of my grandparents' lives were spent in nursing homes. My mother's mom—we called her "Maw"—had lived with my aunt and uncle for many years before her deteriorating health required that she be placed where she could receive nursing care. Maw always had a twinkle in her eye, and she loved to kid around. Both Mother and my aunt visited her virtually every day, sometimes more than once, during the years before she died.

During their final year or so, both Grandmother and Grandfather Hawkins had to be placed in a nursing home. Dad played a key role in this, and he and Mother made visiting them a priority in their busy schedules. Seeing their parents age and having to place them in nursing homes was just about the most difficult thing my parents had to face. Yet they never shirked their responsibility to support their parents with their presence, financial resources and whatever else they could provide.

In recent years, we have become much more aware of the growing need to provide care for our parents. That awareness intensified in February 1991. Kathy and I were living in Dallas, and Mother flew out for a week-long visit. We enjoyed a delightful time visiting friends, children and grandchildren, shopping at the huge Galleria Mall, sightseeing around the Dallas-Fort Worth Metroplex and spending many hours reminiscing with Mother.

Mother's Stroke

When she returned home, Mother told my sister Suzi, the next-oldest to me, she didn't feel well. The following Monday, as her condition worsened, Suzi took her to the doctor. Mother's physician, Dr. Olson, immediately admitted her to Brookwood Hospital. "You're having a stroke, Mrs. Hawkins," was her terse diagnosis.

As a result of the stroke, Mother was left with no left-side vision from either eye. She also began suffering significant short-term memory loss. Her days of actively driving around the Birmingham area were over. Before long she would be forced to give up her decades-long role teaching Sunday school at Westwood Baptist.

The previous year Mother began having hearing and balance problems. The diagnosis was Munier's disease. A few years ago she was given a battery of skin tests and was found to be allergic to at least 15 common environmental substances, including newsprint, glue and photographs (because of the formaldehyde used in the developing process).

Mother's health seemed at low ebb as she and Dad approached their 50th anniversary in January 1995. Her dermatologist diagnosed her with pittiriasis, a condition that left her hypersensitive to ultraviolet rays and unable to spend more than a few minutes in the sunshine. A fall in May 1996 led to hip replacement surgery, and even after extensive physical therapy, she is able to walk only with the use of a walker. Often she needs a wheelchair.

Dad's Vision Loss

While mother's health deteriorated, Dad continued to do well. Since she was unable to drive, he became the primary "chauffeur" for their frequent trips to the doctor, the grocery store and other errands, including regular trips across town to the Homewood YMCA for physical exercise and hydrotherapy.

Although he had lost most of the vision in his right eye in the spring of 1986, Dad had excellent sight in his left eye. In fact, for most of his 42 years as an engineer on the Southern

Railway—now the Norfolk Southern—he had never needed glasses.

Then one morning in May 1995, Dad awakened and felt, as he put it, "like I had sand in my eye." A hastily arranged appointment with Dr. Lanning Cline, one of the top ophthalmologists in the southeast, led to an initial diagnosis of macular degeneration. Dad told the doctor, "It is as though I'm looking at a clock and everything between the three and the six is blank." After a series of tests, Dr. Cline concluded that the smaller nerves around the eye had been damaged because of a lack of circulation. For a time surgery was considered, but as Dr. Cline explained to Dad, "Within just the past month, we've concluded that those who have the surgery actually wind up worse off in most instances than those who don't. If we had operated you might have lost all your sight and been totally blind."

As it was, my sister explained, "Dad's legally blind. He's lost eighty percent of his ability to see."

Status Questions

As my plane landed, I looked over the series of questions I had written down, questions to help determine what needed to be done for Mother and Dad. How are they doing now? What do they need? What are they willing to do?

The following morning I met my two brothers and my two sisters for breakfast in the coffee shop in the hotel where I was staying. Since I wasn't scheduled to speak until noon, we had some time to discuss Mother and Dad's condition.

First we reviewed the significant facts. They still live in the same home on Arcadia Road where I grew up. When it was first built almost 50 years ago, it was a small, two-bedroom home without indoor plumbing, located on a dirt road in the country. Today, after extensive remodeling, it's become a moderately sized, three-bedroom, two-bath home on a suburban corner. Obviously, it's where Mother and Dad prefer to continue living. Whenever the subject of assisted living or a move to a retirement facility comes up, one or the other of them—usually both—will express their preference to stay at home.

However, we also recognized and considered the difficulties, even dangers, inherent in their continuing to live at home. Since neither can see very well, it's quite difficult to keep up with chores around the house. Dad takes care of most of the household responsibilities such as cleaning, since he is better able to move about. He washes dishes, takes out the garbage, even takes care of the laundry and the mopping and vacuuming. But since he can't see very well, he often misses a lot. We're also concerned about the danger that they may forget to turn off one of the burners on the stove.

A few months ago, Mother, who has difficulty getting into the tub, tried to bathe while Dad was resting. She fell into the tub—fortunately the bottom was cushioned with some dirty clothes they had placed there—but she was stranded for nearly three hours! She called out, but Dad, who is hard of hearing because of his years operating diesel locomotives, was unable to hear her cries. Eventually he awakened, went to check on her and found her in the tub, unable to get out. Dad was forced to call 911 and have a rescue team remove her. She was shaken but otherwise unharmed by the experience. But we didn't want to see something like this happen again.

We also discussed the fact that both parents, although generally in good spirits, had experienced some depression because of their losses. In addition, Mother's physician indicated the possibility of beginning stages of Alzheimer's, as evidenced by her increasing short-term memory difficulties.

Mother's physician had arranged for a nurse to make an in-house visit once a week to check on her condition—especially helpful since she takes approximately 16 medications per day. In addition a nurse's aide, a delightful woman named Eartha, came in three times a week to assist Mother with her bath. During the time I spent with them over the weekend, I discovered that Becky had set up a notebook from which Mother and Dad, working together, could keep track as Mother takes her various medications, including an anti-depressant. Becky's husband, Tommy, had given Dad a watch last Christmas with a feature uniquely suited to him—press a button and it gives the time audibly. Four times a day, he and Mother carefully work through her list of medicines, documenting the exact time she takes each tablet. One medication even has to be ground up and taken in three teaspoons of applesauce.

Care Options

Part of our discussion as siblings ranged over the variety of living options—assisted living, extended care, etc. Yet we all realized that, if possible, the most desirable choice was to keep Mother and Dad in the familiar surroundings in which they had lived for so long. But how could we ensure their safety and well-being?

We decided to investigate the possibility of a security alarm. Paul would contact several companies to determine whether one might have an option of a remote, which Mother could carry like a pager, to be used in case she fell or couldn't rouse Dad. Our preference was that she have a device that could sound an alarm and also dial 911.

The second decision we made was to seek someone Mother and Dad would be comfortable with, perhaps someone they already know, who could come in once a week to clean. We decided to check into several professional cleaning services, but we wanted to find a Christian woman who could make sure things were clean around the house as well as provide a bit of encouragement and cheer for Mother and Dad.

I brought up what I considered to be one of the best potential sources of help—Westwood Baptist Church. The little church where Mother, Dad and I had been baptized in 1952 had grown to a membership of approximately 2,000. The senior pastor, Cecil Sewell, and his wife, Sharon, had become very close to Mother and Dad, visiting them in the home on several occasions as well as when Mother was hospitalized. Although they are unable to attend church as regularly as before, Dad still attended about half the time. A member of his senior men's Sunday school class, Charles McCreary, called at least once a week to check on them and ask if Dad or both of them needed a ride to church. On occasion Mother felt able to attend; most often, however, she stayed home. Since the services are televised, they were able to continue feeling as part of the church, and Mother had telephone contact with a number of her friends.

Kathy From McCalla

Although my plan had been to contact Pastor Sewell that Saturday, he was out of town. With his help I had hoped to find a prospective, part-time housekeeper, since I had volunteered to take the initiative on this.

That Sunday I was scheduled to speak at McCalla Bible Church. Mother and Dad felt well that morning, so I picked them up and we drove out to McCalla together.

We saw many old friends there, and we met Clarence and Kathy Bahlmann. Clarence is a student at Southeastern Bible College, and Kathy and Mother seemed to hit it off perfectly—in fact, they must have talked for 10 or 15 minutes after the service.

Just before we were to go to lunch with our long-time friends Tom and Ilona Dyson, it occurred to me that since Mother and Kathy Bahlmann had gotten along so well, perhaps I should approach her about our need for someone to provide cleaning and encouragement. Kathy expressed interest and a willingness to pray about the possibility, and we agreed to make contact again soon. Since Mother brought up Kathy's name several times afterward, I couldn't help thinking that perhaps it was best that I wasn't able to contact Pastor Sewell. After all, we had prayed that the Lord would lead us to just the right person to provide this additional care.

Long-term Strategy
For the short term, the bases seemed covered. Paul volunteered to check on the alarm system, and I offered to pursue the cleaning service. John often takes care of handyman needs, along with Paul, and both Becky and Suzi provide transportation and check on the folks regularly. We decided the only thing left for us to discuss was our long-term strategy.

After discussing issues ranging from our parents' feelings to what might happen if their health continued to deteriorate, we determined our first step would be to consider a "live-in" person to care for them as an interim step before considering a move to an assisted-living facility. Whatever happened, we agreed to respect their dignity, wishes and freedom while doing everything we could to protect them, physically and otherwise.

Thanksgiving in Lincoln
Two weeks later, my parents flew to Nebraska for their first visit since we moved here from Texas four years ago. Mother had been extremely anxious about flying, and we had arranged wheelchairs for her and Dad, which proved extremely helpful during their plane change at Chicago's busy O'Hare International Airport.

Mother's first words to me were, "Thank you all, and everybody else, for praying. I didn't feel any anxiety whatsoever." Since she takes anxiety medication for an obsessive-compulsive disorder, we were all delighted at how well her trip had gone.

Their visit gave us an opportunity to take them to a special pre-Thanksgiving chapel at Back to the Bible, where they were able to meet Dr. Kroll for the first time—they are both avid *Back to the Bible* listeners and supporters. We spent Thanksgiving with four generations, as two of our three children and three of our grandchildren were able to enjoy the occasion with them, and we were able to add to the memoirs we had begun recording in previous visits—a process we hope to continue in future visits.

When I helped them into their seats for their flight home, Mother's comment was, "I can't believe how well this has gone. This has been a wonderful time."

Since none of us knows how long we will have our parents, I couldn't have agreed more.

THE 4
Biblical Mandate

As the years pass, the relationships between us and our parents undergo dramatic changes. We've navigated the transitions from childhood to adolescence to adulthood, modifying our relationships with Mom and Dad as we go. We've enjoyed, perhaps for decades, an adult-adult relationship. Perhaps our parents live just down the street or across town. They may be thousands of miles away, across the country in our mobile society—or they may live in our own home.

There comes a time, however, when we begin to notice a decline in their well-being. They require an increasingly larger amount of our attention and care. They need our help, even seek our advice.

We knew they would get old, but when we first notice Mom's unsteady gait or receive word about Dad's heart attack or Mom's stroke, suddenly we are forced to face the fact that our parents are mortal.

Then comes the biggest shock of all—the individual who always looked after you now needs your help.

You didn't plan for it—no one, at least up until now, seems to have planned to take care of aging parents. But as we move into our 50s and our parents turn 70 or 80, an increasing number of us face this incredible challenge.

Many of us stumble when the roles are reversed and we find ourselves parenting those who were our parents. It's hard to admit that our parents can no longer be trusted to balance their checkbooks or take their medications. Of course, there is a natural reluctance to intrude into another adult's personal life. In addition, old power struggles with our parents, even emotions from our own childhood, can be resurrected at this point. We'll say more about this in a later chapter. Yet all these factors can make this relationship with our elderly parents one of the most challenging transitions in our life.

A Decline in Health

Judy and Dave Hansen first began to notice her parents' health decline just about the time her younger brother died of skin cancer. "Gary's death was a big blow to them in many ways," Judy says. "He was the only one of the five of us who was able to help with the farm work. He was a school teacher, so he had spring vacation to come and help Dad with planting. Then off and on during the summer he would come, and he was always available for harvest. . . . I don't think Dad's ever been able to really completely come to grips with Gary's death." Judy's brother was only 36 and left a wife and two small children.

Coupled with the emotional blow of losing their adult son, Judy's parents both suffered significant physical problems. "Mom was already having trouble with circulation in her feet and loss of eye sight," says Judy. "Both of them are diabetics, but Dad had been generally healthy. We noticed him losing his eyesight—he wasn't able to renew his chauffeur's license. That was a big blow for him because financially, driving a school bus provided the steady income they needed with the ups and downs of farming. Also, with his eyesight deteriorating, Dad was unable to continue the electronic repair work he did on the side.

"Then he began having kidney function problems. In fact, the week my brother died was when my dad went on dialysis and had his name placed on the kidney transplant waiting list.

"We were up there just a few months ago to help my parents get ready for harvest. It was a big shock for me to see how much both my parents have deteriorated health-wise, as well as keeping things up. Since then Mother has suffered a car accident, and Dad, who had a kidney transplant in the spring, wound up back in the hospital with complications. Since Mom's accident was a result of a diabetic coma, her driver's license was revoked, so we had to move my parents into an apartment in town, at least for the time being."

The Distance Factor

Like the Hansens, Janet and Roy Miller live hundreds of miles from Janet's parents. "I've really been aware of Mother's problem for less than a year, but she's progressed to the stage now where we are talking about putting her in a nursing home sooner rather than later," says

Janet. "My brother, who lives near her, has been meeting with an attorney as well as with a physician to find out all the legal issues that need to be cared for."

Janet's mother is 78, and the stress of caring for her and their 85-year-old father has taken its toll on Janet's brother, Tim. As she explained, "He's borne most of the brunt of it. He and my older sister Shirley, who lives in Illinois, have taken most of this on their shoulders. But it's a burden for all of us."

Janet's mother has been diagnosed with Alzheimer's—although as Janet reminded us, "I guess the definitive diagnosis doesn't come until the autopsy." "My mother is still alive, but it's like she's not there any more. I've had to come to terms with that," she says.

"In addition, it's tough because my dad won't really seek out any kind of support, and my brother and sister-in-law have been so busy taking care of their children, working with AWANA and their church, and now they're taking care of Mom and Dad as well. We've all done what we could from a distance. I know we are responsible. The Bible doesn't give us a lot of detail on what or how much to do, but it does tell us to take care of our parents."

Paul's Instruction

Scripture makes it clear God expects us to care for members of our family. In 1 Timothy 5 the apostle Paul provides instructions to a pastor, Timothy, on how the church is to deal with those who are growing older. Paul's opening exhortation urges believers to treat those who are aging with respect. "Do not rebuke an older man, but exhort him as a father, . . . the older women as mothers" (vv. 1-2).

Unfortunately, growing numbers of older Americans are being neglected, battered and financially exploited by their children or other caretakers. According to federally funded research by the National Center on Elder Abuse, reports of domestic abuse against elderly Americans increased from 117,000 in 1986 to 241,000 in 1994. According to the center, less than 10 percent of the nearly two million annual cases of elder abuse are reported.[1] Another study that focused on nursing home personnel revealed that 10 percent have physically abused patients by shoving, pinching, grabbing or slapping them.

According to Fernando Torres-Gil, assistant to the U.S. Health and Human Services Secretary for Aging, seniors are "embarrassed to admit that a relative, a loved one, or a child is abusing them either physically or financially, or neglecting or exploiting them."[2] Clearly such behavior runs counter to the commands of Scripture.

The Bible is explicit, however, that children have a mandate that extends beyond not abusing their elderly parents. As Paul pointed out in 1 Timothy 5:4, "If any widow has children or grandchildren, let them first learn to show piety at home and to repay their parents; for this is good and acceptable before God." According to these clear-cut instructions, the first line of provision for aging parents, including widows, is the immediate family—children and grandchildren.

Verse 8 is even more explicit: "But if anyone does not provide for his own, and especially for those of his own household, he has denied the faith and is worse than an unbeliever."

From this verse we can draw three principles. First, caring for aging parents is a requirement for every believer. We are all to provide for our own. While government programs and outside aid can help, this is a responsibility that ultimately doesn't rest on Social Security or Medicare. Nor is this mandate just for the wealthy or those who can afford it. The word *anyone* indicates each of us has a responsibility to care for family members as they grow older.

Second, the word *provide* actually indicates advanced planning. The implication of this compound term in the original language used by Paul is that caring for aging parents demands careful forethought and planning. Financial counselors have drilled into us the importance of planning our finances in order to be able to put our children through college, purchase a home or retire. This passage indicates another important item that must be included on our list of financial planning matters: caring for parents as they age.

Recently we asked financial consultant Tom Teckmeyer, president of Teckmeyer Financial Services, whether any of his clients had specifically included care for aging parents in their financial planning. Tom, whose clientele includes many Christians, responded that such advanced financial planning was almost non-existent based on his experience.

Tom and his wife, Lori, decided almost a decade ago to set up a parental care fund and began saving for the day when they might have to care for their parents. As Tom explained, "My folks took care of us. One day I know we'll need to take care of them. I wish more people would see the value of this," he added. "I only have one client who's taken this step."

Finally, nothing less than our Christian testimony is at stake. Paul's words are as pointed as the proverbial ice pick. We are guilty of worse behavior than pagans when we fail to care for our parents. As the apostle John writes, "Whoever does not practice righteousness is not of God, nor is he who does not love his brother" (1 John 3:10). When we fail to demonstrate love and care for those who raised us, how can we claim to be demonstrating love for God?

Clear Principle, Complex Dilemmas

Despite the clear-cut nature of Paul's instruction in 1 Timothy and the New Testament application of the "honor thy father and mother" principle from the Ten Commandments in Ephesians 6:2, the application to our various circumstances raises complex dilemmas. The following is a list of several important issues to consider.

First, independence is an important value to us all. Everyone—including our parents—would like to enjoy the freedom to make our own choices so we can experience a fulfilling life.

"Mother and Dad can't continue living at home," Cynthia asserted. "That's the third time in three months I've come over and found a stove burner on. They'll set the house on fire. I'm going to have to insist that they sell their home and move into an assisted-living facility."

"I'm taking Dad's keys," Bob declared. "Last week he almost ran over the child next door! Plus he's had two fender benders in the last six months. Just because he's too stubborn to admit he can't see well enough to drive doesn't mean I should let him kill somebody."

These may seem like clear-cut situations. Yet the reality is our parents have lived independently for many years. Now impairments threaten to encroach their freedoms, compounding their stress and ours. They may need more help around the home with cleaning, cooking, taking out the trash, paying bills or shopping. Trips to the doctor may increase, and they may require transportation on a regular basis.

A second issue involves physical and mental well-being. As our bodies age, their functions deteriorate. Sometimes the loss is gradual. On other occasions it may occur suddenly. Just walking about or climbing stairs becomes more difficult. Infections may take longer to heal. Parents may become incontinent and experience the shame of a lack of bladder control. Elderly people are at greater risk of a fall, which results in much more serious consequences, including hip and knee replacement surgeries. Arthritis and other kinds of joint pain may increase from occasional and mild to chronic and severe. Cancer becomes a greater risk, and even routine checkups may uncover life-threatening physical problems.

Mental stability also becomes a factor. While some individuals retain a sharp, clear mind, others often begin experiencing memory loss and confusion over simple things. Forgetfulness is not just a symptom of Alzheimer's disease; it can have other causes as well.

Senility

The term frequently used for the decline in mental and physical abilities is *senility*, which comes from a Latin word meaning "old or old man."[3] The simplest definition of senility is "the loss of physical and mental ability that occurs with advancing age." According to Elizabeth Loftus, a psychology professor at the University of Washington and an authority on memory, "The typical senile man or woman can usually recall past events of information that has been stored in long-term memory before senility sets in. However, there is a disruption of ability to store new information. Thus, the present slips away while memories of the past linger."[4]

According to David Wechsler, who developed the Wechsler scales of intelligence, and other authorities, some memory or cognitive loss is simply a consequence of the aging process. Yet many experts such as John Horn argue that performance in some kinds of memory situations may weaken a bit with age, while other intellectual abilities can actually increase. In addition, such factors as education, health and work environment can play a part in a person's ability to exercise his cognitive skills.[5]

While studies may show conflicting evidence, the fact is many people do suffer memory impairment in later life. Those of us who are responsible for caring for our parents often have to deal with their forgetfulness and confusion.

Coupled with the physical and mental decline is a frequent increase in emotional instability. Part of this is due to the fact that a lot of emotional agitation is linked with loss, which leads to grief. While everyone experiences losses, older people often experience greater losses. More loved ones, friends and family members die. Medical and financial pressures loom large. Our parents may have fewer emotional resources to cope with these circumstances, plus mental confusion and communication difficulties may produce anger. As a result, they may begin to feel overwhelmed with hopelessness and depression. In addition, certain forms of cancer and other physical disorders can cause clinical depression, increasing emotional instability and reducing whatever resources may be present for coping with life's changes and losses.

Financial Pressures

Financial issues provide another important dilemma. As our parents grow older, their income may become fixed or decline. These days many breadwinners find themselves pushed into early retirement because of corporate downsizing and other workplace changes. Often our parents are forced into a quick adjustment from being a two-income family to a single-income one, or even left with the fixed income of retirement. Another factor may be the death of a spouse.

Often our parents refuse to face the reality of adjusting their standard of living. They may insist on continuing a previous lifestyle for which they have no ability to pay. Or they may make unwise decisions about finances, purchasing an expensive car or house or taking that dreamed-of vacation.

Add to these factors the onset of skyrocketing medical bills, stir in a generous dose of fear of destitution—after all, many of our parents survived the Great Depression—and finances can pose an incredible dilemma. Many of us would like to help our parents, yet we find ourselves faced with limited resources to handle our own financial responsibilities, which may include putting one or more child through college.

A Mobile Society

A final dilemma involves the mobile society in which we live. Some elderly people have large, caring families who live nearby. Several children may have ample resources between them; or some may have money while others have time. Responsibilities may be shared, leaving no one overburdened.

On the other hand, since two out of five families move each year, many parents live far from their children. Both of us are examples of this, since we live thousands of miles from our parents, who reside in Pennsylvania and Alabama. Though we make it a point to keep in touch with frequent telephone calls and visits, there is still a keen sense of physical separation.

In other families the distance may be more emotional than geographic. Or it may be both. One of us has been friends for many years with a couple who raised an only son. They are all Christians and have been active for years in a local church. When the son married, he and his wife at first lived in the same city, just a few miles from his parents. They felt they would never lack for their son's love and attention.

A few years later a career opportunity prompted the son and his wife to move to another city. The parents were concerned about the distance, especially since they had no other children, yet they felt his ongoing love and concern would overcome that obstacle. Within a few years, however, he began to express indifference toward them, then anger, claiming he was unhappy with the way they had raised him. Sadly, this couple missed much of their grandchildren's lives, plus the encouragement and help of their only son and daughter-in-law—all because of this geographic and emotional distance. While their local church pitched in to help meet their needs, emotionally and even physically at times, theirs was a tragic situation.

Sometimes when our parents live far away or become incapacitated, we may face the question of moving closer to them or having them move in with us. Should we uproot them from familiar surroundings, their dwindling number of friends and homes where they have lived? Or should we uproot ourselves and perhaps our own children, changing careers or ministries in order to position ourselves closer to our parents to help them?

Spiritual Implications

All these issues—physical, emotional, mental and financial—have spiritual implications. Scripture makes it clear that God is concerned about the well-being of each of us. As Paul prayed in 1 Thessalonians 5:23, it is the desire of the God of peace that the whole of each of us—spirit, soul and body—be "preserved blameless at the coming of our Lord Jesus Christ." He is the God of grace, who promises to give wisdom to those who ask Him in faith (James 1:5). He can provide wisdom and extraordinary grace for every situation related to parent care, including our own emotional responses to the dilemmas they face.

[1] Andrew Weaver and Harold Koenig, "Uncovering Elder Abuse," *Christian Ministry*, July/August 1997, pp. 18-19.

[2] "Abuse of Elderly Thought Rising," *The Lincoln Star*, May 2, 1995, p. 3.

[3] Elizabeth Loftus, *Memory* (Reading, Mass.: Addison-Wesley Publishing Co., 1980), p. 103.

[4] Ibid., p. 104.

[5] John W. Santrock, *Life-Span Development*, 4th edition (Dubuque, Iowa: Wm. C. Brown Publishers, 1992), pp. 590-598.

OUR 5
Emotional Response

Moses was one of the most remarkable individuals to walk across the pages of history. When he died, Scripture record that "Moses was one hundred and twenty years old . . . . His eyes were not dim nor his natural vigor abated" (Deut. 34:7).

Most of us like to think our parents possess that same indestructible, undiminished youthful vigor. When we are confronted with our parents' finiteness, when we must face the inevitability of their aging and their mortality, however, we are often left in an emotional turmoil.

"I just can't handle it," Karen lamented to her pastor. "Mother and Dad have always been there for me. Anything I've needed, they've provided. Now she has Alzheimer's and doesn't even know who I am most of the time. And he's wrapped up in his own world and doesn't even respond when I ask him for help."

Karen's dilemma helps us understand our own emotional responses to the aging of our parents and their need for our care. Remember, emotions are simply responses to a situation, a crisis or an ongoing source of stress, such as caring for aging parents. While we characterize some people as more "emotional" than others, even the most stoic individual must come to grips with anger, fear, worry or envy.

Our purpose in this chapter is not to explore in detail what Scripture says about emotions—that would require an entire book in itself. Instead, we want to consider emotional responses to what's happening to our parents and the demand their situation may place on us for care. Also of concern is how the past affects our present responses, and how we may slip into old patterns of emotional interaction with our parents. Gaining insight into these may help keep us from wrong and unproductive responses to a need for caring for our parents.

Denial and Anger

Perhaps the initial and most common response to the aging of our parents is denial. It's a very common way to avoid looking at the truth about their circumstances and our feelings about them.

"I don't see why you're making such a fuss about Mother and Dad," Walt told his brother and sister. "After all, they're still in good health. Sure, Dad has trouble seeing, but so do a lot of other people on the road. He has more than enough experience behind the wheel to compensate for slower reflexes or the lack of vision, and he does wear glasses. And Mother—I don't think there's a chance she has Alzheimer's. She's always been a little forgetful and scatterbrained. I think you're just trying to make them old before their time."

Walt's arguments sounded plausible, but coming as they did in the face of clear evidence from his mother's physician and his father's driving record, they could best be described as denial.

Scripture clearly warns of the danger of denial. The apostle John wrote, "If we say that we have no sin, we deceive ourselves, and the truth is not in us" (1 John 1:8). At the heart of most denial is self-deceit—according to Jeremiah 17:9 it is the deadliest condition of the human heart.

Yet denial is a common response to parental aging, especially when Alzheimer's is present. Writing to explain how she and her family responded to her husband's diagnosis with Alzheimer's, Lela Knox Shank explained: "The first stage of the disease could be called the 'denial' stage, for both the patient and the family, since the patient in the beginning is still able to take care of all his or her personal needs and generally to continue living a normal life. In fact the patient is often well into the first stage of the disease before the family knows anything is wrong. Yet all the while these early symptoms are stealthily creeping in, changing the personality of the patient." [1]

As Shank so clearly points out, denial is often a mask for another common emotional response—anger. We use denial as a defense because it's painful to face our feelings.

The Anger Response

Anger and fear are perhaps the two most basic emotional responses we experience. Both are responses to threats, real or perceived. Students of human behavior have long recognized the "fight or flight" response to whatever threatens our well-being.[2]

Why would we feel angry because our parents are growing older and need our help? The answer is clear. Ever since we were infants our parents represented that final line of defense against a hostile world. We may have become mature adults, raising our own families, but we still feel that sense of "well, if things turn really nasty, I can call on Mom and Dad—if not for tangible help, at least for advice and encouragement."

Suddenly we are faced with our parents' mortality. No longer can they help us. Instead, they need our care. The roles have been reversed, and our own security and esteem may be at risk. The natural response of fallen humans to this kind of threat can be anger. Or it can be fear.

"I'm doing everything I can to help my mother," Louise explained to her pastor. "But it never quite seems to be enough. Mother's in constant pain, and she's always unhappy. I feel so sorry for her."

"How about you?" the pastor gently asked. "How are you doing as her caregiver?"

"Fine," Louise responded, then she paused for a moment. "Actually, I feel sad for both of us, to be honest about it. And sometimes I get really angry about how my life is all wrapped up in hers. Then I feel guilty for being so selfish. After all, she took care of me when I was a child.

"I guess the bottom line is I feel trapped. I can't fix her problems. I can't make her happy. But I have to be there to help. I don't even have time for my own husband and children."

In addition, we may feel angry toward our siblings for refusing to help as much as we expect. And if our parents have been placed in a nursing home or extended-care facility, we may feel angry toward those who are caring for them for not providing a level of care we think we would provide.

Dealing With Our Anger

Scripture makes it clear that all anger isn't sin; however, Paul's clear guidelines for dealing with anger must be applied to our emotional responses to our parents' situation. These guidelines are found in Ephesians 4:26, 31-32: "'Be angry, and do not sin': do not let the sun go down on your wrath. . . . Let all bitterness, wrath, anger, clamor, and evil speaking be put away from you, with all malice. And be kind to one another, tenderhearted, forgiving one another just as God in Christ also forgave you."

The first step in dealing with this emotion is to break through denial and face the reality of our anger. The term Paul used for "be angry" literally means to become angry or face our angry feelings. We can never handle anger in an appropriate or godly fashion if we refuse to examine it in our own hearts.

Second, it is important to respond to our anger quickly and without sinning. This is why Paul urged us to deal with anger before sundown—bedtime in the culture of the first century. That's why he also called on us to put away bitterness, rage, arguing and slanderous speaking, along with ill will.

Finally, we must decide to forgive. This includes forgiving our parents for growing older, for no longer being able to help us and for needing our help. We also must choose to forgive siblings and others who fail to meet our expectations when it comes to providing for our parents. Above all, God's provision of forgiveness for us in Christ must always be our standard of extending forgiveness to others.

The Fear Response

In many ways fear is the opposite of anger. If anger is our "fight" response, fear moves us to flee. Just as with anger, it's a response to a threat to our existence or well-being.[3] Fear is the first emotion mentioned in Scripture. Immediately following his act of disobedience, Adam admitted to God, "I was afraid because I was naked; and I hid myself" (Gen. 3:10). While little children fear the dark, grown-ups fear all kinds of disasters, including situations for which we do not have strength or wisdom.

David addressed these sources of fear in Psalm 27 when he wrote, "The LORD is my light and my salvation; whom shall I fear? The LORD is the strength of my life; of whom shall I be afraid?" (Ps. 27:1). David affirmed that, even though an army might be encamped against him, he would not permit his heart to fear (v. 3). Furthermore, he recognized that even if his parents abandoned him "the LORD will take care of me" (v. 10).

Psalm 27:10 has direct and significant implications for parental care. In a sense, our fearful feelings may be a response to perceived abandonment. After all, our parents are no longer capable of providing the things we received from them throughout our lives. They're just not there for us any longer—they can't be. Since they need us to be there for them, we may feel abandoned and suffer the grief of loss.

Closely related to fear is worry or anxiety, another emotion about which Scripture speaks at great length. The term used in the New Testament for worry actually has the root meaning of "to be distracted." It's an accurate picture. When we become worried about or preoccupied with something, including the care of our aging parents, we are no longer able to give full attention and energy to other priorities of life.

Yet the word for worry can be used in a positive way. For example, the same word translated "be not anxious" in Matthew 6:25-33 is used of Paul's care for the churches (2 Cor. 11:28) and of the care Timothy and Titus extended to the people they served (2 Cor. 8:16; Phil. 2:20). It was also used of the care provided by the innkeeper because of the efforts of the Good Samaritan (Luke 10:34-35).

Yet clearly there are times when we need to be distracted from life in order to care for others, including aging parents.

The problem comes when we allow that distraction to draw us away from our focus on the Lord. That's why in Matthew 6:25 Jesus warned His listeners against the distraction of material things or preoccupying concerns about the future. Instead, He urged them to seek first His kingdom and righteousness (v. 33). In essence, the bottom-line issue when it comes to worry is trust. That's why Jesus pinpointed the problem with the words "O you of little faith" (v. 30).

So our emotional response to our parents' situation boils down to a matter of trust. Can we entrust our parents and their needs to God and His provision? Can we trust the Lord for grace to obey, to fulfill our responsibility to care for them? Or will we be stalled by denial, overwhelmed by anger, paralyzed by fear or distracted by worry and anxiety?

Echoes From the Past

Many of our emotional responses in the present grow out of memories, patterns and responses that were part of our relationship with our parents as we grew up. We've all heard stories about childhood regression, children wetting the bed under stressful circumstances or teenagers throwing the kind of tantrum a three-year-old would be proud of when denied the right to a car. Perhaps you've also felt those strange emotions expressed by Lena, a woman from Maine who phoned our radio ministry to say, "I just can't go home to my mother any more. She constantly tries to run my life. I'm married and in my forties, but whenever I walk through the door of that childhood home it's just like I'm a child again—to me and to her."

This same emotional confusion can hinder us from providing the kind of mature care our parents need at this stage in our lives and theirs. It's imperative to guard against such childlike emotional responses.

For some, the immediate problem may involve a return to childhood rebellion. Perhaps our "pattern" involved rebelling against our parents and their instructions. If that's the case, we may respond to the present situation by refusing to provide the help they need. If so, we must heed the instruction of Scripture established in the

Ten Commandments and repeated by Paul in Ephesians 6:2 to "honor your father and mother." After all, rebellion and honor cannot coexist.

A second common response we must be careful of involves childhood obedience. Perhaps we were conditioned to obey without question. For children this is a totally appropriate response. After all, Paul commanded in Ephesians 6:1, "Children, obey your parents in the Lord, for this is right." Now that we have grown into adulthood and our parents have entered their second childhood, however, the obedience relationship should be superseded by an adult-adult relationship involving honor. This also may mean at times we need to relate to our parents based on the general principle found in 1 Thessalonians 5, where Paul writes, "Warn those who are unruly, comfort the fainthearted, uphold the weak, be patient with all. See that no one renders evil for evil to anyone, but always pursue what is good both for yourselves and for all" (vv. 14-15).

Clearly there may be times when our parents need a firm, loving word from us—always given in respect—when they place themselves and others at risk. At those moments we must put aside the baggage from the past and deal with the problem in the present.

The Trust Issue

As we survey these emotional responses to our parents' need for care, one bottom-line solution comes to mind. It's the one David advocated in Psalm 37. When life doesn't seem to be going right, when God doesn't provide instant solutions and you're unable to figure out what's going on, David offers this simple response: "Trust in the LORD, and do good; dwell in the land, and feed on His faithfulness. Delight yourself also in the LORD, and He shall give you the desires of your heart. Commit your way to the LORD, trust also in Him, and He shall bring it to pass" (Ps. 37:3-5).

David's simple, straightforward answer involves trusting the Lord. Elisabeth Elliot expressed it clearly in a recent edition of her program *Gateway To Joy*. She described a phone call from a 60-year-old mother whose daughter owned the house she lived in. This woman's daughter refused to let her mother have company and told her mother she should start looking for a retirement home. Elisabeth offered this analysis of the daughter's unwillingness to care for her mother:

"Fear governs so many of our decisions, doesn't it? Are you afraid you can't care for your mother? Oh, probably the truth is you can't. But if it's what God is calling you to do, He'll see to it you can. Trust Him. Cast all you cares on Him."[4]

Elisabeth's own experience caring for her mother in her declining years was documented in her little book *Forget Me Not*. In it she writes, "We find mother tiny but erect in her wheelchair with perhaps a book or letter in her lap. The expression of perplexed sadness on her face gives way instantly to astonishment and delight when she sees us. Up go the arms, so unbelievably thin you think they'll snap if you hug her. Well, we hug her as well as we can in her wheelchair.

"'Where have you been?' she says. 'I've been here a week and not one of my six children has been to see me. Nobody comes near me. Oh, please get me out of here.' We explain that we've been to see her many times, and the other children, so have they. She doesn't believe us. We explain that we all live a long ways away.

"'Why did you move so far away from me?' she wants to know. We tell her that she moved away from us. She lived first with one son and then with another. She denies this and then concedes that perhaps we're telling her the truth. She hopes we are, but she doesn't remember. . . . Conversation is almost impossible. We try asking questions. What did she have for lunch? They didn't give her any lunch she says. We try to tell her about her great-grandchildren. It's all news to her. The names of even her grandchildren are strange. . . . She asks why our father has not been to see her not even once since she came to the hospital. We remind her that he has been with the Lord for twenty-three years. 'Why, nobody told me,' she says bewildered at our carelessness.

"We read a few words from the Bible, ask if she remembers about the everlasting arms. She says she does, and we pray with her. She prays too. She can still do that and sometimes we sing. It's amazing how well she remembers the old hymns."[5]

The story of Elisabeth Elliot's mother provides a graphic, touching reminder of how strong our emotions can be when we face our parents' need for care.

For Elisabeth, remembering that her mother was still a part of the Body of Christ, that God had purpose in her sufferings, that her mother certainly didn't want to be a burden, left her convinced of the imperative of trust.

"But I don't understand," you say. We are not asked to understand. We are asked simply to trust Him.

[1] Lela Knox Shank, *Your Name Is Hughes Hannibal Shank: A Care Giver's Guide to Alzheimer's* (Lincoln, Neb.: University of Nebraska Press, 1996), p. 16.

[2] For a fuller discussion of these emotions, see Dan Allender and Tremper Longman III, *The Cry of the Soul* (Colorado Springs, Colo.: NavPress, 1994), pp. 44-53.

[3] For a comprehensive discussion of fear, see Don Hawkins, *The Roots of Inner Peace* (Grand Rapids, Mich.: Kregel Pub., 1996), pp. 105ff.

[4] Elisabeth Elliot, *Gateway To Joy*, Oct. 13, 1997.

[5] Elisabeth Elliot, *Forget Me Not* (Lincoln, Neb.: Back to the Bible, 1997), n.p.

WHAT 6
To Do

An old Dutch proverb says, "We get too soon old and too late smart." Without question we all need wisdom to know what to do in providing care for our parents as they grow older.

While Scripture speaks clearly and specifically to some of the issues related to caring for Mom and Dad, on others it is silent. We are told to honor our parents (Eph. 6:1) and to plan in advance to provide for their needs (1 Tim. 5:8). Yet nowhere does Scripture tell us that we should or shouldn't move them into our own homes or place them in a retirement facility or a nursing home.

In this chapter our goal is to provide some practical action steps that may help you deal with your parents' increasing need for care, based on some of the principles we have considered.

Myths and Misconceptions

One thing we need to be careful of is avoiding the common myths about aging. Some of these were documented by Bert Kruger Smith in *Aging in America*. For example, it is a myth to believe that older people cannot learn. We may chuckle over the folk saying, "You can't teach an old dog new tricks." But people aren't dogs. Another myth is that older people have no interest in sexual intimacy. Scripture points out that Abraham, Sarah and Boaz, among others, still maintained the physical intimacy of married life.

A third myth is that older people do not want to work. While many people may have pointed their energies toward retirement, many physically able persons prefer to work beyond the customary retirement age, not just for the income, but because they want to feel needed and useful. Other myths include the following: older people like to be helpless; older people prefer to spend their time with other older people; older people are forgetful and have lost touch with their previous talents.

A final misconception is that older people have settled their personal and spiritual accounts. Clearly, as some people grow older, they become more and more consumed with bitterness, harboring grudges and reliving past hurts. Even many Christians have given themselves to bitterness. We need to give every effort to help guide them to choose to forgive, based on the forgiveness God has extended to us through Christ.

Others who are up in years still need to settle that most basic and important issue of a personal relationship with Christ.

Ernie was a cheerful 91-year-old resident of a New Jersey retirement center when he chose to attend a conference in Bermuda where I (Don) was speaking. An energetic, talented, former professional musician, Ernie never ceased to amaze his fellow travelers with his physical energy (one day he walked more than two miles), his talent at playing the piano and his cheerful disposition.

Yet Ernie had never come to the place in his life where he recognized his need of a Savior and placed his trust in Jesus Christ. Less than three days into the conference, during a personal conversation with one of the trip leaders, Ernie acknowledged his need, bowed his head and invited the Lord Jesus to give him the gift of eternal life. Near the end of the week he told me, "I'm learning a lot this week—I've even read about a third of your book."

The lesson of Ernie's experience is obvious. It's never too late for a person to come to faith in Jesus Christ.

Tough Choices

Life is sometimes filled with tough choices. For Marvin and Donna Carr the decision for Donna's mother to enter a nursing home was far more difficult than when they invited both parents to live in their home. As Marvin explained, "My wife and her brother are the only children. They talked this over and felt it was best for them to be some place where they could be cared for rather than our simply going to their home with a meal every day or something like that." But after Donna's parents moved to the Carrs' home, her mom's condition deteriorated. Increased medical problems, including arthritis, led to her decision to move to the nursing home.

"It was a tough decision," Marvin explained. "Everyone in the family had to exercise patience and understanding. It took a lot of prayer too."

Donna's mother could have the advanced care she needed, while her 93-year-old father continued living with the Carrs.

Several incidents brought Cherry Thompson and her siblings to the conclusion that advanced care was necessary for their mother. According to Cherry, "She moved to Lincoln in 1972 after my dad died. She did well for a long time. It's one of those tough things when you watch your parents age—especially when the physical health isn't really all that bad, but the mind starts to go."

According to Cherry, her mother underwent extensive testing for Alzheimer's at a Lincoln-area hospital. "They concluded that there was a lot of depression, so we couldn't be sure, but the general assumption was that she had Alzheimer's or some version thereof."

Several incidents provided a catalyst for placing Cherry's mom in a nursing home. "For a long time she was living in an apartment," Cherry says. "She never actually lived with us. But I would go over two or three times a week. One Saturday I went over to do her hair, and she looked at me in a funny way and said, 'Did you see Mother and Dad?'

"I thought, 'What's going on?' and I said, 'No, should I have?' She said, 'Why not? They were just here. They were coming to take me to go somewhere.'

"At that point I knew we were in trouble.

"Later my brother came down from Omaha and stopped in to see her, and Mom wasn't in her apartment. She had gone across the street to a park, and when he asked her why, she said,

'They told me I had to move out.' Fortunately it was the summer. If it had been winter . . . .

"At that point we decided something definitely had to be done. My three brothers met with my sister and me to discuss the options. At first, my sister Jean came down from North Dakota, and she and I took turns staying with Mom. That lasted for about a month. My sister had gone through the process with her father-in-law. She insisted that none of us even consider trying to take care of Mom, with all her needs, in our home. It was a difficult process trying to get Medicaid approval, because we couldn't afford the nursing home, and she certainly couldn't. It's really tough because you feel like in a way you are sneaking around behind your parent's back. But there was no way we could tell Mom what we were doing. We didn't lie to her; we just didn't discuss it with her. She had so few coherent moments, she would never have understood what her children were deciding.

"My oldest brother was living in Indiana at the time, finishing his training at Grace Seminary. We all persuaded him to be the one to tell her the final decision about the nursing home, since he was the oldest son. Four of the five children were there when we placed her in the nursing home."

When we face hard decisions like Donna and Marvin Carr and Cherry Thompson, we definitely need direction. Fortunately, we're not left to our own resources. As God promised through David, His Word is designed to function as a lamp to our feet and a light to our path (Ps. 119:105).

In view of this fact, and the Scriptural exhortation to honor and care for our parents, what practical steps should we take?

Practical Steps

First, we need to pay close attention to changes in our parents' lives. Since both of us live some distance from our parents and generally see them a couple or three times a year, we're usually able to spot changes pretty quickly. For adult children who live nearby, however, changes in their parents may be more gradual and harder to notice. Look for signs like failing memory, a weakened ability to get around, tendencies to leave stove burners on or water running, or difficulty keeping up with housecleaning or personal hygiene.

Second, it's important that we recognize the variety of issues our parents face. For many, especially those who have lost a spouse, loneliness is a major factor. For many others health becomes a primary concern. Medical problems can range from Alzheimer's to cancer, from dementia to depression. For still others the major pressures may be financial.

Third, it is essential that we choose to forgive our parents for any wrongs they may have done us. This means following biblical instructions not to hold grudges. Perhaps our parents neglected us in the past, favored our siblings or even abused us. The only option that pleases God and helps maintain our own spiritual and emotional well-being is to choose to forgive them. This also includes choosing not to become bitter over any impositions their circumstances may place on us now. It's tempting to resent the demands and pressures of parent care, but it will help if we remember all the Lord has done for us, and even the things they have done for us in the past.

Frequently, both parents and children need to process long-held bitterness. Recently "Beth" called our radio program to express her concerns over a bitter, angry mother-in-law. "She's sixty-two and facing heart surgery," Beth said. "How do I handle her bitterness?"

We encouraged Beth to extend and model the forgiveness we have in Christ based on Ephesians 4:32. We suggested she gently encourage her mother-in-law to discuss the issues of bitterness and forgiveness, to continue maintaining contact with her mother-in-law and keep showing love in tangible ways. Above all, we used Luke 18:1 as a basis for urging her to continue praying for her mother-in-law and not give up.

Fourth, when facing the tough decisions demanded by the needs of aging parents, it is important to seek wise counsel. This includes questions such as, "Do I take Mom and Dad into our home, hire someone to stay with them, or try to get them into a retirement facility?"

Another radio listener, Joan, phoned to talk about her 75-year-old mother who was in relatively good health but who seemed paranoid over the prospect that she might be placed in a nursing home. Joan and her husband had been discussing whether or not to move in with her mother. We encouraged her to talk with her pastor about the issue, and to survey resources to see what was available in her community. These days there are so many options available, including assisted living. Often people can be hired to do household chores, provide lawn care and help with transportation to the doctor or the grocery store.

A fifth action step involves recognizing the value God places on the wisdom of age. Our society today has come to view aging people as less productive, less beautiful, less energetic, more forgetful, perhaps even of less value. Yet the psalmist pointed out that "those who are planted in the house of the LORD shall flourish in the courts of our God. They shall still bear fruit in old age; they shall be fresh and flourishing, to declare that the LORD is upright" (Ps. 92:13-15).

All of us who are involved in ministry, including local churches and media ministries, must avoid the temptation to limit our efforts to the young and the hearty. As the senior segment of our population continues to grow and their problems increase, we must provide compassionate, biblical help on a wide range of issues. As a Christian community, we cannot allow the secular world to set the pace in serving those who are in the "home stretch" of their life spans.

Perhaps part of the problem involves our own fear that the end is drawing near. In the words of Horace Deets, executive director of the American Association of Retired People, "It is understandable that the generation of baby boomers who had such a difficult time passing thirty, think that the end is near when they turn fifty. But the truth is, turning fifty no longer has the same significance in the life cycle it once did. In fact as a friend of mine recently said, 'Half a century ain't as old as it used to be.'"[1]

Sixth, when you are forced to make a difficult decision, pray about it, seek counsel, then make the decision without regrets. It's always important to count the cost of any option, as John Gillies points out in explaining how he and his wife cared for two aging parents. "Home care is a glorious proposition, but it is costly—in dollars and cents and in energy and life-style."[2] Sometimes the best option is to move parents into your home. Or it may be more important to provide additional care where they are, even if it requires remodeling or renovating the home where they have lived for years in order to allow them to remain there.

Whatever decision you make, trust God to guide you as you seek His wisdom. But be sure to avoid the traps of second-guessing and guilt-tripping yourself.

Recently, a woman from California wrote to advice columnist Ann Landers:

"After my father died, my brothers and I knew that my mother would be unable to cope by herself in her big house. Although they discussed modifying their own homes to accommodate Mother, I was very strong in my opposition to this. I told them there was no way Mother could live in my home without destroying my marriage. And I suspected the same was true for them. They eventually agreed and [we moved] Mother into a facility where she could get more and more attention as her physical and mental abilities deteriorated. . . .

"Every time I visited her I felt guilty. Did she rub it in? Of course. 'How can you make me live in a place like this?' she would ask. But after I left I knew that this was the best solution for a bad situation. Mother had better care in that facility than my family or I would ever have been able to provide.

"I realize this may not be the best answer for everyone, but it was the best one for us. It was a tough decision but I've never regretted it."[3]

Clearly this woman's decision is not the right one for everyone. But apparently it was right for her. It was the same decision Elisabeth Elliot and her family reached regarding Elisabeth's mother (see chapter 5). Whatever the option, it's important to make the decision with prayer, wise counsel and a mind saturated with the principles of God's Word.

For Judy Hansen and her brothers and sisters, distance was a big factor—that and their parents' inability to safely maintain their preferred life on the farm. "My dad was one of five brothers," explains Judy. "My grandfather homesteaded the land, and each of the brothers had their own land. My dad would be the first one to actually have to give up his land. That's really difficult, since he spent his whole life working that land and hoping it would continue in the family. Since one of my brothers has died and the other one isn't in farming, I think the past few years have really been difficult, especially for Dad.

"Neither of them can drive now. We want them to have their independence, but on the other hand, we can only visit them a couple of times a year. When Mom had the accident this fall as a result of a diabetic coma and Dad was in the hospital with complications from his kidney transplant, the doctor decided not to release them unless there was someone to stay with them.

"It was a difficult decision, but we chose to place them in an apartment in town. There was simply no other way for them to get transportation to shopping or anything, and Mother has had to go to the hospital several times this past year because of diabetic reactions. The doctor felt it would be better for her to be in town rather than living on the farm ten miles away.

"We made it a point not to push them to make any decisions about closing up the house or selling the farm. They certainly weren't in favor of moving to town, but the day after a big snowfall, Dad told me on the phone, 'I looked out the window this morning and saw all that snow and realized I didn't have to go out and shovel the sidewalk.' That was the first positive word from him about moving into town. Of course, his dream is still to go back to the farm."

Finally, whether your parents live in your home, their own home or a retirement or extended-care facility, it's vital for the children (and grandchildren) to visit as often as possible and let them know they are not forgotten. Spend time with your parents. Take a tape recorder along and record their reminiscences. After they're gone, you will be thrilled that you've made those tapes.

Most important, the love and honor you will be extending to your parents through your regular personal contact will help you fulfill your God-given responsibility to provide Christlike parent care.

---

[1] Horace B. Deets, "Invitation from A.A.R.P. is not the end," *Modern Maturity,* July-Aug. 1997, p. 82.

[2] *A Guide to Caring for and Coping with Aging Parents*, John Gillies (Nashville, Tenn.: Thomas Nelson, 1981), p. 89.

[3] Ann Landers, "Haven't Regretted Putting Mom in Home," *Lincoln Journal Star*, Sept. 2, 1997, p. 8B.

TRAPS 7
To Avoid

While neither of us was a world-class athlete, we both enjoy sports, particularly football. After all, it's hard to live in the home of the perennial-champion Nebraska Cornhuskers without enjoying an occasional gridiron contest. Recently our entire state paused to acknowledge Tom Osborne as he retired after 25 years as head coach.

One of the reasons Coach Osborne's Nebraska football teams won consistently every year is because they developed an excellent running game. For years the team has ranked at or near the top for moving the ball on the ground, usually averaging well over 400 yards per game—an amazing figure.

Two of the most effective running plays used by the Huskers are the option and the trap. On the option the quarterback has to choose the right runner to carry the ball—should he hand it to the fullback, keep it himself or pitch it to the trailing tailback?

The other effective play is the inside trap. Every football defense, including the Cornhuskers, must learn how to avoid it. On a trap, the defensive man rushes in thinking he's about to make a big play—perhaps a tackle behind the line of scrimmage. Suddenly he finds himself blindsided out of the play by one of the offensive linemen.

In similar fashion, those of us with parents who need increasing care as they grow older may find ourselves susceptible to one or more traps.

In this final chapter we want to talk about seven common traps we often fall for when we are trying to care for our parents. The list is not exhaustive; you may think of others. But if you aren't careful, even the wise among us may fall for one or more of these traps.

The Denial—Delay Trap

Those who fall into this trap generally have parents who have been relatively healthy and independent. Their thinking is, "I have plenty of time. There's no need to worry about this yet."

While we don't advocate worry, we do encourage planning. In an earlier chapter we considered the meaning of the word *provide* in 1 Timothy 5:8. Paul's concept is clear. The term means to plan in advance.

Not only is a failure to plan for parent care unbiblical, it can actually lead to serious consequences. For example, you may find yourself forced to make quick, uninformed decisions about medical or financial issues. You may have difficulty trying to locate community services as you deal with a crisis in the making, or even find yourself in court trying to secure the legal right to manage the care of a parent who is too confused or ill to make decisions for himself.[1]

The first step is to sit down and have a serious talk with your parents about their situation. Where would they prefer to live if they were unable to continue in their home? Could they afford nursing home care? What about issues like aggressive medical intervention? Would they prefer to have someone in the home with them? Would they rather live with you or with some of the other children?

When you hold the conversation, make sure your parents have an up-to-date will, complete with any additional instructions concerning life-sustaining medical care, plus a durable power of attorney. This simple legal document gives you or someone else the right to manage your parents' financial and personal affairs should they be unable to handle them. It is particularly important should both parents become disabled at the same time.

This may not be an easy conversation to hold, but it's a great place to apply the biblical principle of "speaking the truth in love" (Eph. 4:15). And it's the proverbial ounce of prevention that can head off many pounds of trouble.

Remember that speaking the truth in love involves tact and diplomacy, essential ingredients for respect. Make it clear that you wish to respect your parents' desires, but you need to know what they are. Then instead of immediately expressing your opinions, listen carefully. James 1:19 reminds us of the value of being "swift to hear, slow to speak, slow to wrath."

Sometimes the best approach may be to use the strategy of raising an issue with regard to yourself or someone else. For example, you might ask, "What do you think of the Life Care

Center that Uncle Tom and Aunt Bonnie moved into?" or, "I had my will revised a few weeks ago. I was wondering if yours is up-to-date."

If your parents are reluctant to discuss the issues, don't force them to. But if their situation becomes pressing, then ask siblings or other relatives, a pastor, perhaps a physician or lawyer, to join you in intervening.

The Rescue 911 Trap

One of the easiest traps to succumb to and the hardest to overcome is the feeling, "I must rush in, rescue my parents and do everything for them." Some of us seem to relish taking a "Rescue 911" approach to problems because it can make us feel good about ourselves and make us look like heroes to others.

However, this trap poses two dangers. First, when you try to bite off more than you can chew, you jeopardize your own physical, emotional and spiritual well-being, as well as damage other important relationships in your life. Second, trying to assume the hero's mantle is one of the surest ways to wind up feeling resentful about all you have to do in comparison with others, and guilty over the fact that you can't do more.

The appropriate thing to do is set limits. That's what Jesus did. When He and His disciples faced the pressures of meeting the needs of a multitude during a period of intense ministry, the Lord's instruction was to "come aside by yourselves to a deserted place and rest awhile" (Mark 6:31). Jesus clearly understood how easy it is to respond to the needs of others without recognizing our own limitations. That's why He set limits for His disciples. While sacrifice and compassion are important Christian virtues, we also have to understand our own limitations. You certainly can't make your father well, protect your mother from future risks or make their relationship with each other better.

Cherry Thompson recalled her older sister's insistent wisdom. "When things were going downhill with mother and we knew she couldn't stay in the apartment, we talked about all the options, including moving Mother into one of our homes," she says. "Jean had been through this with her husband's father. She insisted that we not even consider trying to take care of Mom in our home. It turns out she was right."

Judy and Dave Hansen wrestled with the same issue and came to the same conclusion. "I wish we were closer, and it was easier to get there," says Judy. "They live in eastern Montana; you have to fly into Billings, then drive six hours to get to their home. It's a sixteen-hour trip by car from Lincoln, and of course, in the winter it's practically impossible. We talked to my parents to see if they would be willing to move down to Lincoln at least for the winter and live with us. They definitely didn't want to move in with any of the kids right now. They'd rather stay where all their friends are. Dad says, 'Why would I want to move to a city where I don't know anyone?' Dad wants to be in a small town or out in the country, so we've tried to honor that. The problem is that none of us kids are really close, so it puts a burden on everyone, including family, extended family and the church family. We had to consider what we could do—and what we couldn't."

Marvin Carr explained that he and his wife, Donna, have worked hard at making her dad feel like part of the family. "We offer to take him with us to a lot of church activities and other things. Sometimes he wants to go; sometimes he doesn't. We respect his decisions, to go with us or stay home. We fixed up one of the rooms in the house for his use. Sometimes he helps me in the yard, raking leaves, picking up sticks, that sort of thing, plus he helps with setting the table and doing the dishes. He can't do a lot, but it helps him feel like a useful, contributing member of the family."

One of Judy Hansen's major concerns is to avoid infringing on her parents' turf. "I've noticed my dad can't make decisions as well now as before," she says. "Part of that is due to the medication he's taking. Sometimes it may seem easier to make the decision and do it yourself. I know that's not good for them, but on the other hand, they do need our input, our help.

"We want them to have their independence. When I'm there I'd like to feel like I'm being useful. It's hard to find the balance. I don't want to treat them like I feel they can't do things any more. I want to be careful not to just take over for them. I think that would rob them of their dignity."

Perhaps it would be helpful to make a list of things you can and can't do. Are there repairs around the home you could do to make things safer? Are you able to provide financial guidance, perhaps write checks and pay bills for parents who can't see as well? Can you provide transportation to the doctor? Perhaps you can call or visit on a regular basis.

One thing you can do is enlist the help of others. Frequently there are neighbors, church volunteers, siblings or other relatives or friends who can help meet needs. One of the things I (Don) have been able to do for my parents is coordinate and encourage help from brothers and sisters, members of the church family, long-time neighbors Tura and Wallace Davis, several volunteers from Westwood Baptist Church, Aunt Carolyn and other friends. My sisters have coordinated community services, including the delightful woman named Eartha who comes in three times a week to help Mother bathe, the man who cuts the grass and those who help clean the house.

For Cherry Thompson, supportive family and friends provided the necessary help for that difficult time. "My really long-suffering, patient, kind husband put up with a lot and was very encouraging," she says. "My friend Dawn Leuschen from Back to the Bible was incredibly helpful. She listened to a lot of my gripes and tears, was always patient with me, and would stand in for me when I had to leave work and rush over to the nursing home. I don't think you can make it without supportive family and friends."

For some people the answer is a geriatric care manager, a professional who helps oversee different aspects of the care of aging parents. In any case, it's important to remember that a burden shared is always half a burden.

The Resentment Trap

One of the greatest dangers when parents need care is the threat of jealousy and conflict among brothers and sisters. Sometimes childhood rivalries resurface, or new conflicts develop. If one child winds up shouldering most of the day-to-day care, he or she may resent the fact that the others aren't more helpful. Those who live at a distance may feel guilty about their inability to be involved regularly, and irritation may develop between them and those who live close.

Part of the answer to this involves ongoing, open communication based on the biblical principle of speaking the truth in love. This not only means communication between children and parents but among all of the children. Sometimes a family meeting is in order. Such meetings can range from an informal discussion over coffee or breakfast to a structured formal meeting that includes a pastor or family counselor. If some of the children live out of town, the meeting can be planned for a holiday when everyone is home. Another option is to arrange a conference call.

There may be times when it's best not to have your parents present. At some point, however, they must be included in the discussion, unless they are incapacitated, since the object is to focus on their current and future needs.

These meetings may be difficult, but try to keep the discussion going. Don't overlook the resource of a pastor and a local church in mediating and resolving conflicts that grow out of resentment among siblings, or between adult children and parents.

The Take-charge Trap

Sometimes our parents reach the point where they have virtually given up and want us to take over. You may wind up like Kay, who has to dress and feed her mother, then take her to senior day-care. When you are driving your parents to the doctor, tying their shoelaces or purchasing adult diapers, you may begin to feel like you are now the parent. But even though a measure of role reversal has taken place, you're really not the parent.

Granted, there will be times when you need to speak the truth in a respectful yet forceful way. Some time ago a friend had to take the car keys away from his father, who had been involved in several accidents and had become a danger on the roads, yet refused to stop driving. However, this friend was careful to talk things through lovingly with his dad and mother and include his sisters and brother in the discussion.

After all, your parents are still your parents. Most important, they are the Lord's creatures with a right to be honored and have their needs, opinions and preferences respected. As aging authority Dr. John Reed said on one of our radio broadcasts, "There's nothing more important you can give your parents than your honor and respect."

Personal understanding also can go a long way. For example, if your mother has died, but your father refuses to move out of a large house and into a senior residential complex, try to understand why he feels the way he does. You may be straightforward yet respectful as you point out the reasons you think he should make the choice to move. You may enlist your pastor, siblings and others to help persuade him.

If he's mentally competent and still refuses to budge, you may have to accept his decision and arrange to have someone visit him regularly, perhaps live in the house or arrange for a meal delivery program.

It can be tempting to try to seize control when we're caring for our parents. It's a mistake we need to take care to avoid.

The Indecision Trap

The opposite of the previous trap, this one involves failure to take action or make the tough decisions when it's time to do so. It's an extension of the first trap we discussed—denial. Suddenly a situation has confronted you. Your father has been diagnosed with Alzheimer's or is legally blind, or your mother has had a stroke. The situation demands that tough decisions be made—and soon—but you and perhaps your siblings feel paralyzed, frozen into inaction. What can you do?

First, and yet frequently forgotten, is the all-important resource of prayer. You may respond, "Isn't that obvious?" Yet it's amazing how many times we've seen, in the heat of a crisis, adult children plunge in, list options or take simply the first available course of action without consulting the Sovereign Creator of the universe.

Our purpose is not to develop a full-blown understanding of prayer here—other books for that are available.[2] But both of us have found that important decisions should never be undertaken without spending significant time away from the press of circumstances and in the presence of the Lord. In addition, this is a great time to enlist the church family, friends in other parts of the country and believers at work to pray for wisdom and grace.

Second, seek wise counsel. Don't feel like you have to make the decision on your own. Although God has given every believer the indwelling Spirit, He has also given us each other. Proverbs 11:14, 15:22 and 24:6 present in clear detail the benefits of seeking wise, godly counsel from multiple sources.

Finally, after praying, spending time in the Word, waiting on the Lord and seeking wise counsel, make your decision, implement it and don't second-guess yourself. God has promised to provide us with wisdom when we ask in faith (James 1:5). Trust the Lord, take action, then count on Him to work things "together for good" (Rom. 8:28).

The Martyr Trap

One of the great dangers facing anyone who cares for their parents is to say, "My needs are unimportant." This becomes trap number six— the martyr trap—which might be described as the Rescue 911 trap on steroids. Remember, when you provide hands-on care, you must carve out time for yourself. Whenever you find yourself saying, "I'll take time for myself later; right now Mom and Dad need me," you're headed for trouble. After all, if you become sick, worn out or even depressed, as frequently happens with caregivers, how will you be able to serve your parents? Caring for an aging parent can be frustrating, painful, exhausting, even overwhelming, but there are resources available.

Look for volunteers in the community or church, or other relatives who can fill in, even for a brief time. If necessary hire someone. Check on senior day-care programs.

Make sure you take some time just for yourself to meet your physical, emotional and spiritual needs. In addition, resist the temptation to cut off contact with good friends. You may feel like you can't take the time, but their support is invaluable.

Finally, look for the treasure. You will receive benefits from the care you are giving. Providing care for parents demands sacrifice. The process can be irritating, yet even irritations, pressures and sacrifices can have benefits.

Two of the most beautiful substances in all creation are the diamond and the pearl. According to geologists, diamonds are produced as great pressure is exerted on certain forms of carbon over an extended time. And most of us are familiar with the oyster, and how the irritation of a particle of sand causes the creature to secrete layer after layer of what ultimately hardens into the beautiful pearl.

Glenda Revell is a friend of our ministry. We met her through Elisabeth Elliot. Throughout her childhood, Glenda suffered a series of incredible abuses at the hands of those who should have loved and protected her. Then, after the Lord provided her with a loving husband, she suffered two miscarriages. As Glenda said, "His hard lessons had not been wasted on us. Our Father's wise discipline yielded the fruit of peace and thankfulness . . . . Meanwhile, we discovered that our dear Father had been reserving His best for us."[3]

Glenda, now the mother of four beautiful children, further explains, "God has performed an infinite act of grace, giving me beauty instead of ashes, crowning with lovingkindness and tender mercy my redeemed, overflowing life."[4] If Glenda Revell can suffer the extensive abuse and adversity of life and come out with an attitude like this, certainly we can find the treasure and benefit in the adversity we experience.

The Perspective Trap

The final trap for us to consider involves the danger of losing perspective. By now your parents may seem like a shell of their former selves. They've become helpless—and you're responsible. You dread the thought of remembering them as they are now. You wish you could preserve only the memories of the time when they were robust, healthy and mentally sharp.

That's where adopting Paul's eternal perspective is important. If your parents know the Lord, they are standing at the threshold of eternity. As Paul reminds us, we hold the treasure of life in "jars of clay," so we'll depend on God (2 Cor. 4:7, NIV). That's what the apostle implies when he continues "...to show that this all-surpassing power is from God and not from us." Even though our human tendency is to attempt to handle life's challenges on our own, the Lord has graciously built in limitations that draw us away from self-reliance to trust.

The apostle's experience bears out the fact that we can expect adversity on every hand (vv. 8-9). Yet he affirms that because of our trust and hope in the Lord, "All things are for your sakes" (v. 15), providing grace to come through every trial with an attitude of thanksgiving.

For this reason he urges us not to give up (v. 16) but to claim God's grace every day. After all, he points out, "our light affliction, which is but for a moment, is working for us a far more exceeding and eternal weight of glory, while we do not look at the things which are seen, but at the things which are not seen. For the things which are seen are temporary, but the things which are not seen are eternal" (vv. 17-18).

None of us can fully grasp the significance of eternity. The comparison between a drop of water and a vast ocean doesn't begin to do justice to the difference between time here and eternity with God. That's why it's important to not simply focus on parent care, but on the eternal implications of our present situation.

---

[1] For a more comprehensive discussion of this and several other of the issues discussed in this chapter, see Virginia Morris, *How to Care for Aging Parents: A Complete Guide* (New York: Workman Publishing, 1996).

[2] See *Empowered to Pray* and *When God Doesn't Answer*, Woodrow Kroll (Grand Rapids, Mich.: Baker Book House).

[3] *Glenda's Story*, Glenda Revell (Lincoln, Neb.: Back to the Bible, 1994), pp. 113-114.

[4] Ibid., pp. 121-122.

ADDITIONAL
Resources

Alzheimer's Association
919 North Michigan Avenue, Suite 1000
Chicago, IL 60611-1676
(312) 335-8700
www.alz.org

American Foundation for the Blind
11 Penn Plaza, Suite 300
New York, NY 10001
(800) 232-5463
www.afb.org

Arthritis Foundation
1330 West Peachtree Street
Atlanta, GA 30309
(404) 872-7100
www.arthritis.org

Elderhostel
75 Federal Street
Boston, MA 02110-1941
(617) 426-8056
www.elderhostel.org
(Offers educational adventure programs for retirement-age individuals throughout the world.)

Food and Drug Administration
Public Affairs Office
P.O. Box 15905
Lenexa, KS 66285
(913) 752-2120
(Information on food, drug, cosmetics, health and medical devices.)

Meals on Wheels
(Contact your local hospital to see if this program is available in your area. It provides one meal a day for home-bound adults at a nominal cost.)

National Consumers League
1701 K Street, N.W., Suite 1200
Washington, D.C. 20006
(202) 835-3323
www.natlconsumersleague.org
(Since 1899, NCL's three-prong approach of research, education and advocacy has made it a highly effective representative and source of information.)

National Eye Care Project Helpline
(800) 222-3937
(Offers ophthalmological care to U.S. citizens and legal residents age 65 and over who have not been receiving medical attention. Provides the name of a volunteer ophthalmologist who will treat the patient at no cost.)

National Fraud Information Center
P.O. Box 65868
Washington, D.C. 20035
(800) 876-7060
www.fraud.org
(Among other services, this agency provides video programs to seniors, their families and groups on how to combat fraud and victimization of elderly consumers.)

The inclusion of any program, Web site or organization is not meant to imply an endorsement by the authors or Back to the Bible.